# Non-Fiction Titles by Janvier T. Chando
ICONS AND VILLAINS: Recent Political Assassinations…
FALLEN HEROES: African Leaders Whose Assassinations…
UKRAINE: The Tug-of-War Between Russia and the West
Cameroon: The Haunted Heart of Africa

# Fiction Titles by Janvier Chando
The Usurper: and Other Stories
Triple Agent, Double Cross
Disciples of Fortune
The Union Moujik
Flash of the Sun
Fortune Calls
Fortune's Master
The Girl on the Trail
Fortune's Children
The Norilsk Bears
Me Before Them
The Grandmothers and Perfect Love
The Fire and Ice Legend
The Sweetest Madness
The Hunger Fire
The Shades of Fire
Father and Sons
Fateful Ties
The Verdict of Hades
His Majesty's Trial
Ngoko's Folly
The Usurper
The Dowry
I am Hated
The Oaf

# Upcoming Titles by Janvier Chando
The Home Drifters
The Mortal Friends
The White Hawk
The Norilsk Bears

# Darkness over Ivory Coast (Cote d'Ivoire): Laurent Gbagbo's Case as a Lesson for the rest of Africa

Janvier Tchouteu

TISI BOOKS

NEW YORK, RALEIGH, LONDON, AMSTERDAM

PUBLISHED BY TISI BOOKS

www.tisibooks.com

# Acknowledgement

Thanks to the Cameroonian Diaspora whose difficult situation has served as a source of inspiration for this expression of what awaits our beloved Cameroon.

# DEDICATION

This account is dedicated to the loving memory of Dr. Samuel F. Tchwenko, and to our fathers who were patriotic in their words and deeds, and who embraced their compatriots without holding any biases.

# Darkness over Ivory Coast (Cote d'Ivoire): Laurent Gbagbo's Case as a Lesson for the rest of Africa

# Contents


| | |
|---|---|
| Acknowledgement | 7 |
| Dedication | 9 |
| Maps | 15 |
| Quotes | 21 |
| INTRODUCTION | 19 |
| Chapter 1 | 23 |
| Chapter 2 | 25 |
| Chapter 3 | 28 |
| Chapter 4 | 31 |

# MAPS

**Ivory Coast on a map of the world**

# Partition map of Africa (1884-1914)

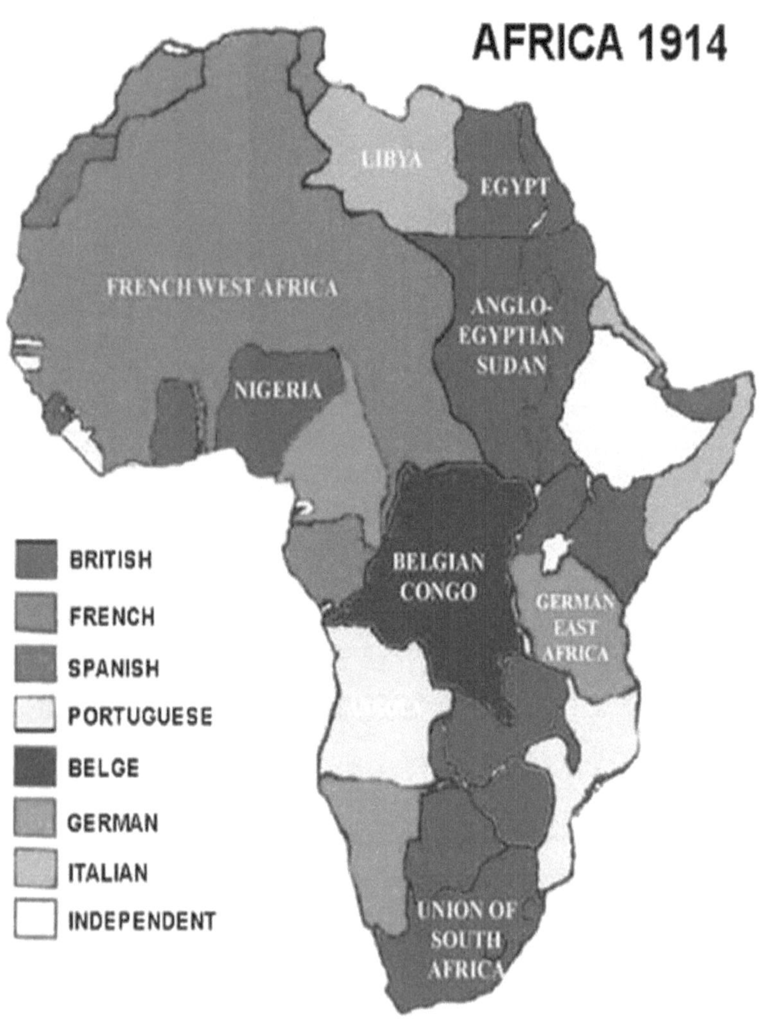

# Political map of Africa

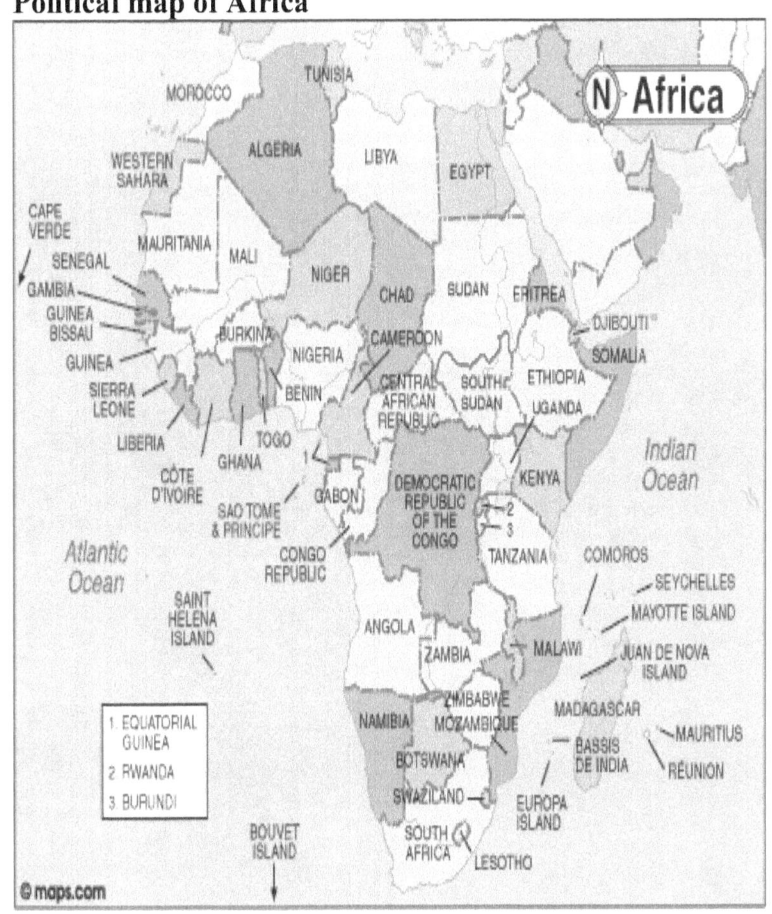

# African Democracy Ratings

# Map of Ivory Coast (Cote D'Ivoire) in Africa

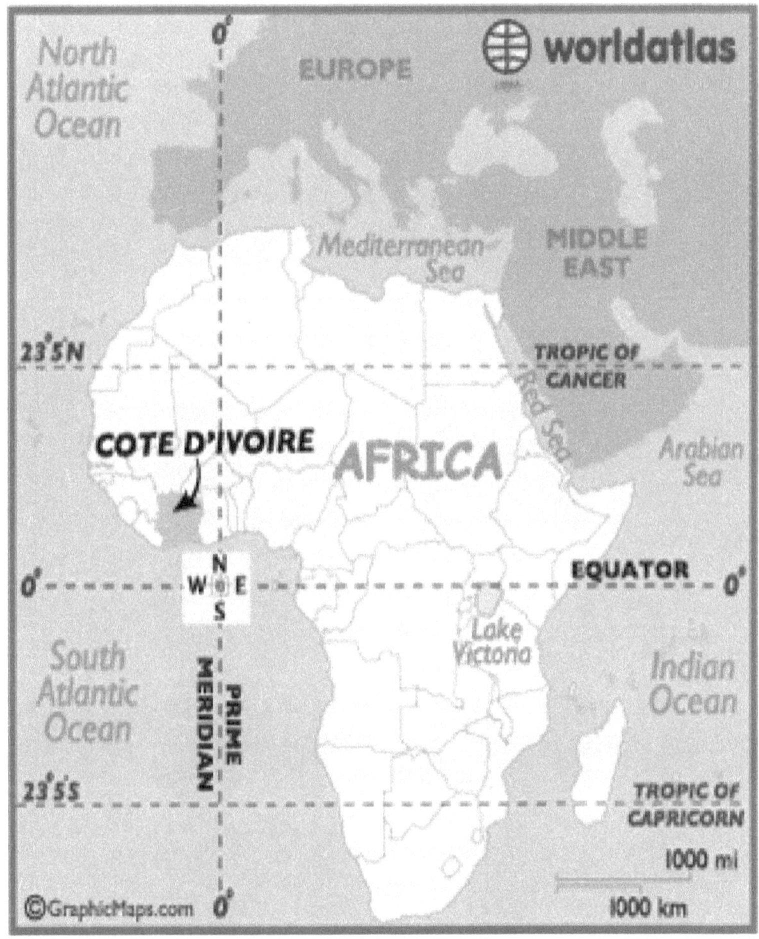

# Quotes

"I will never forget the moment when, for the first time, I felt and understood the tragedy of colonization. [. ..]. Since that day, I am ashamed of my country. Since that day, I cannot meet an Indochinese, an Algerian, a Moroccan, without wanting to ask for forgiveness. Forgive all the pains, all the humiliations that have been made to suffer, that we made their people suffer. Because their oppressor is the French state, that does it in the name of all the French, therefore also, for a small part, in my name. That is why, in the presence of those whom the French State oppresses, I cannot but blush, I cannot but feel that I have faults to redeem myself of."

**- Simone Weil**

"Between colonizer and colonized, there is room only for chore, intimidation, pressure, police, robbery, rape, compulsory cultures, contempt, mistrust, arrogance, sufficiency, Whistling, decrepit elites, degraded masses. No human contact, but relations of domination and submission that transform the colonizing man into a pawn, adjutant, babysitter, chicote; and the native man into an instrument of production. It's my turn to ask an equation: colonization = change."

**- Aimé Césaire**

"Neocolonialism is nothing but a slow and progressive destruction of the emancipation of peoples."

**-Souleymane Boel**

# INTRODUCTION

Many pundits hold that Cote D'Ivoire is the one country in Africa where a neatly blueprinted scheme of French neo-colonial control of Africa was most effectively used, and that it is very difficult to miss the impervious nature of FrancAfrique in that West African county. The seemingly negative connotations of those points of view leave an outsider wondering whether there isn't something beneficial to the country in that aspect of French neocolonialism. After all, Abidjan, the largest city and former capital stands out as a modern metropolis in a continent that lags behind the others; at the end of the day, the country is relatively well-to-do vis-à-vis its neighbors; and for thirty years after independence, this West African nation did not experience political instability.

Ivory Coast, otherwise called Cote D'Ivoire, experienced no political instability for three decades because of its first president Félix Houphouet-Boigny who before and after independence in 1961, made himself and his country a subservient partner of France, Ivorian nationalists with anti-French or patriotic views, hold.

Félix Houphouet-Boigny was a pragmatist, his supporters hold. He knew Cote D'Ivoire could not do without France, and so stirred his country towards a partnership with France that led to development and prosperity, unlike his Guinean counterpart Sekou Touré who broke off all links with France, his supporters hold.

If that were the case, then how come Laurent Gbagbo, the Ivorian civic-nationalist and pan-Africanist who never hid his distaste for French-neocolonialism made it to power after the demise of the Ivorian legend?  And how come it had to take French military intervention to remove Laurent Gbagbo from power?

This succinct account is meant to throw more light on the Ivorian quagmire, an impasse that reflects the ambivalence of French influence in the country, Francophone Africa and the rest of the African continent.

# Chapter One

Often times, the most complicated peace is better than the simplest war. Both Laurent Gbagbo and Alassane Ouattara are losers, and both led the Ivorian people towards a losing path. I pity them both because I think there is a nucleus of goodness in their souls when it comes to their desires and their overall commitment to the wellbeing of Cote D'Ivoire.

There are tons of lessons to learn from the decade-old Ivorian quagmire that ultimately led to the humiliation of a naïve Gbagbo and the crippled ascension to power of Ouattara; one of which is that the arena of African power play or politics is a battleground of ancient Greek classic proportions, like "The Iliad", where the warriors glow in their bravado, unconscious of the external influences of the greater powers (the gods) in their victories, defeats, survivals or escapes. The 1990s generation of the Cameroon Student Movement called *"Parlement"*, especially those of the later years, suffer deeply from that incomprehension, which among other reasons is why the anachronistic French-imposed system is surviving in Cameroon. It is also why the absentee Paul Biya, the French puppet who has been passing around for thirty-eight years as the president of Cameroon easily pulls off masquerades of fake elections that his Western puppet-masters validate by recognizing the false results of these elections.

It becomes obvious from the debacle between Gbagbo and Ouattara that the source of the rift between the two comes from the system imposed by France and their degree of acceptance or allegiance to this system that safeguards France's interest in the country, even above that of Ivory Coast. This French-imposed system makes Ouattara a benevolent mercenary overseeing the management of Ivory Coast and casts Gbagbo as someone who was initially coerced but managed to overcome his inferiority complex into becoming a recalcitrant renegade. Or better put, Ouattara comes across as a glorified comprador and Gbagbo as a flame that cannot be extinguished by his enemies, a firebrand whose victimization exposes the underside of his victimizers all the more.

# Chapter Two

France's detrimental involvement in African local politics especially after it pushed these countries into civil conflicts has been done with impunity. Those involvements are usually masqueraded as French efforts to save lives in areas they controlled in the past and ensured peace and prosperity during their colonial rule. In a nutshell, France and the squabbling successors of Félix Houphouet-Boigny (Henri Konan Bédié, Alassane Ouattara, and General Gei etc.) saw Gbagbo's 2000 electoral victory as an unacceptable mistake on their part that needed correction. Developments in the country after that, whether directly or indirectly, stemmed from that conception.

Countries like Cameroon will never be free unless France accepts the error of its ways one way or the other. And some Africans are not helping the process of growth, the procedures involved in France taking itself out of its entrapment vis-à-vis its lopsided relationship with its former colonies and territories in Africa. As a matter of fact, even though France is viewed internationally, especially among the community of advanced nations as a law-abiding, civilizing and progressive nation, it has been carrying on in its relations with these Francophone nations in a mafia-like manner or like a dehumanized mafia don operating in a clandestine manner and acting with impunity.

In a nutshell, France's behavior in these African countries is like that of someone unconcerned about the welfare of the African people. In fact, it is hard to argue against some pundits who believe that it is outright racist and that it feeds on the minds of bigots who hold the twisted view of the child-like innocence or ignorance of the African. These are people who revel in the delusionary perception of Africans as a people incapable of coming up with anything good.

We would be hard-pressed to find someone with a strong enough argument that it is not a good idea to dismantle the political and economic system France implanted in its former colonies in Africa in the 1960s before granting them independence, thereby nurturing political establishments in those new African countries that protect French interests more than the interests of these new nation-states. Such a process of knocking down the anachronistic system in the different African countries, which in their totality constitutes FrancAfrique, is a process that can be accomplished only by genuine civic-nationalists with the revolutionary drive, pan-Africanist vision, and a deep love for their people. That is why advocates of the New Africa should be chided when they come out blindly against those Africans who in their amateurish and short-sighted ways confronted the full machinery of the conspiratorial powers (or god-like powers when analogizing from ancient Greek mythology) that are undermining the wellbeing of Africa and Africans.

I won't comment deeply on this Ivorian problem. We will face it again in Cameroon; and the rest of Central Africa will be gripped by similar deceptions in the next couple of years. But one thing for sure is that this French pattern has been in application for close to a century in Africa, which is why those in the French political establishment who are directing and managing the political and economic control of Africa, especially the system of control of Francophone Africa (FrancAfrique) view FrancAfrique as a successful template and a winning strategy that does not require changing.

# Chapter Three

The job of the advocates of change of the post-independence generations is to study the methods of control employed by foreign powers that are keeping Africans under perpetual helplessness and chaos to the point where the organizers of the chaos end up looking like the saviors. Africans should understand their history, master the levers of power, and know that their salvation rests only in them sticking together and accepting one another as indispensable contributors to a future, prosperous and free country, and continent.

I say so with sadness because two days ago, I talked with ex-Zairois who blamed Patrice Lumumba for the deplorable state of The Democratic Republic of Congo today, accusing him of taking Congo to independence when they were not ready, of bringing Mobuto to power, and for failing to share his vision with the other politicians. It is like blaming Jesus Christ for his betrayal by Judas. And

Congo, the sick heart of Africa will find itself trapped for eternity in incomprehension if it does not reconcile itself to its paralyzing history inflicted on the infant nation by the powers that plotted Patrice Lumumba's ouster and death.

Equally, in a three-way discourse with a Dutch professor in Amsterdam in 2003, a fellow compatriot argued forcefully that there has never been a war in Cameroon, that no massacres were carried out by French and Ahidjo forces, that Biya is a great leader, and that Cameroon was doing great, which is why it is better off than most African countries. A fool's paradise I called it. Or was he gripped by the *Potemkin syndrome* at the time? Not until the young man read "Triple Agent, Double Cross" afterward, not until after he had his curiosity aroused and not until after he did some research of his own, did he lament the degree of brainwashing he and most Cameroonians had been subjected to. He was still suffering the effects of the brainwashing he underwent in Cameroon, even while studying and living in Europe's most liberal country.

Africans need to emancipate themselves from the mental slavery that still has most of Africa trapped in incomprehension and suffering from a lack of sense of direction. The lucky ones, especially those in the Diaspora, should be leading the effort of emancipation.


*April 13, 2011*                              *Janvier Tchouteu*